Hearing

First published in the U.S. in 1994 by Carolrhoda Books, Inc.
c/o The Lerner Group
241 First Avenue North, Minneapolis, Minnesota 55401

Copyright © 1993 Wayland (Publishers) Ltd., Hove, East Sussex
First published 1993 Wayland (Publishers) Ltd.

Library of Congress Cataloging-in-Publication Data

Suhr, Mandy.
    Hearing / written by Mandy Suhr ; illustrated by Mike Gordon.
        p.   cm. – (I'm alive)
    Originally published: Wayland Publishers, 1993.
    ISBN 0-87614-833-X
    1. Hearing–Juvenile literature. [1. Hearing. 2. Senses and
sensation.] I. Gordon, Mike, ill. II. Title. III. Series: Suhr, Mandy.
I'm alive.
QP462.2.S84 1994   93-44190
612.8'5–dc20   CIP
                                                                          AC

Printed in Italy by Rotolito Lombarda S.p.A., Milan
Bound in the United States of America

1 2 3 4 5 6 – P/OS – 99 98 97 96 95 94

Hearing

written by Mandy Suhr
illustrated by Mike Gordon

Carolrhoda Books, Inc.
Minneapolis

Listen to the sounds around you.
What can you hear?

Some sounds are quiet and peaceful.

Some sounds are loud
and noisy.

Some sounds make you feel happy.

Some sounds make you feel mad.

Sounds travel through the air, but you can't see them.

You use your ears to hear them.

The outer part of your ear catches sounds and sends them down a hole. This hole leads to a tunnel that goes right inside your ear.

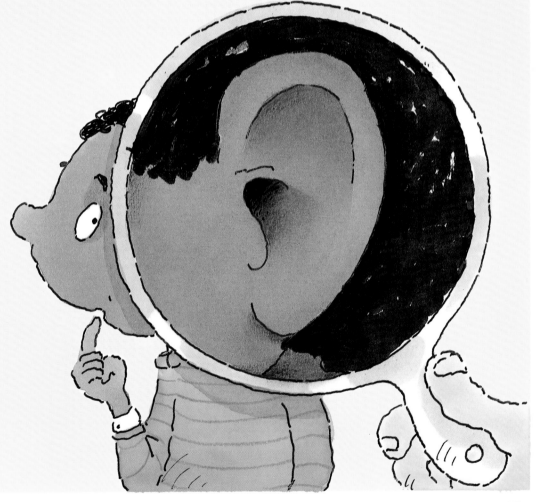

At the end of the tunnel is a thin
piece of skin. The skin is stretched
tight across the tunnel, just like
the skin on the top of a drum.

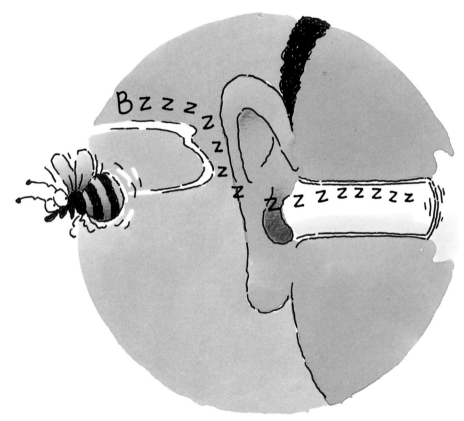

This is called your eardrum.

When sounds hit your eardrum,
they make it wobble, or vibrate, just
like when you hit a real drum.

When your eardrum vibrates, it makes three tiny bones in your ear move.

These little bones send messages through a long, curly tube, called the cochlea, to your brain.

The messages go to your brain along paths called nerves. Then your brain figures out what the sounds are.

RING
RING

Some animals can hear better than people. Rabbits are very good at hearing. They can even move their ears around to help them find out where sounds are coming from.

Dogs can move their ears too. They prick up their ears so that they can "catch" the sounds more easily.

Dogs are very good at hearing. They
can even hear some sounds that
people can't hear.

When you have a cold, you can't hear very well because your ears are all blocked up.

But your hearing soon
comes back as you
get better.

Rachel is deaf. This means that she can't hear very much at all. She wears a special hearing aid that helps her, and she watches people's lips to see what they are saying.

But she's still the fastest
runner in school!

You have to take care of your hearing.
Very loud sounds can hurt your ears.

Some people work in very noisy places. They have to wear hearing protectors to keep their ears from being hurt.

What sounds do
these things make?

Can you copy these sounds? How
many other sounds can you make?

A note to adults

"I'm Alive" is a series of books designed especially for preschoolers and beginning readers. These books look at how the human body works and develops. They compare the human body to plants, animals, and objects that are already familiar to children.

Here are some activities that use what kids already know to learn more about their sense of hearing.

Activities

1. Watch a television show with the volume turned all the way down. Can you tell what the show is about? Can you tell what people are saying by watching their lips? Notice how important facial expressions become when you can't hear the tone of a person's voice.

2. Take your sense of hearing on a walk! Notice loud sounds like a jet flying overhead or children shouting to each other in the park. Notice soft sounds like birds chirping and the wind blowing through the trees. You'll be surprised how many different sounds you can hear if you really listen.

3. How are outdoor sounds different from indoor sounds? You can make a poster that shows indoor and outdoor sounds. Take a sheet of construction paper and draw a line down the middle. Label one side "outdoor sounds" and the other side "indoor sounds." Then look through old magazines for pictures of things that make noise. Cut out the pictures and paste them on the construction paper. You will probably find that there are some things, like dogs barking and people talking, that are both indoor and outdoor sounds.

4. Some words, like "Mississippi" and "zigzag," are fun to say. This is especially true of onomatopoeic words. These are words that sound like the noise they are describing, such as "clap" or "crackle." How many onomatopoeic words can you think of?

I'm alive!

Titles in This Series